Maureen O'Hanlon Freder, MSW

LEAN BACK

Bring Authenticity and Value
To Every Interview

Print ISBN: 978-1-09839-272-7
Ebook ISBN: 978-1-09839-273-4

This book is dedicated to my mother and father for always encouraging me to take just one step in the right direction as it will lead you to a great journey. And to my husband, Bill and three children, MacKenzie, William and Robert for teaching me the vital difference between the words "Talk" and "Act." And to my readers, I applaud you and thank you for taking a bold stance to be the best version of yourself as you bring true value and authenticity to your next interview!

Enjoy,

Mo

INTRODUCTION

I am about to walk you into the mindset of an interviewer. What exactly are they looking for in a potential candidate? Simply put, interviewers are looking for someone who has the ability to perform the job, someone who is prepared and able to convey a polished message and ultimately be a good fit for their team.

My goal with *Lean Back* is to prepare you for any type of interview so that you are hyper focused on sharing your story instead of being nervous. As a result, you can posture yourself to "Lean Back" in your chair and command their attention.

That's right! The focus is on YOU. We are going to dive deep into your mind, body and spirit so that you are prepared, and ready to bring authenticity and value to your upcoming interview. Chances are you are either a recent graduate, changing jobs or looking for *that* promotion. You see what jobs are out there. You make a decision to submit your resume. You must be patient and persistent. Responses don't always come along.

But then it happens! After tens of hundreds of applications submitted electronically, you finally get that call or email to move on to a phone screen, video or a face-to-face interview. In light of COVID-19, you most likely have a video or text interview. The feelings of panic and excitement become indistinguishable emotions. The sheer fact that someone responded from that black hole we call "classifieds cyberspace" sends you reeling into a euphoric state. Then, after that moment settles, you start to think about the "what ifs".

- What if I'm not what they are looking for?

- What if I don't know an answer to one or more of their questions?

- What if I don't have all the experience they are looking for?

- What if I don't get the job?

The "what ifs" are enough to stymie that euphoric feeling unless you approach this thing called "the interview" in a systematic, strategic, and seamless way. You need to know what they are looking for in a candidate but more importantly- yes more importantly- you need to know what YOUR story is. How will you separate yourself from the competition?

Being prepared with your story is just one part of getting that dream job. This handbook will aid in raising your level of sophistication with the interviewing process, and give you a sense of purpose and confidence to *Lean Back* while on the hot seat. I have not only interviewed hundreds of potential candidates but also served as mentor and coach to many people ranging from high school students and college students going for that internship to adults who are looking for a promotion or change of career.

As a former clinical social worker who now works in corporate life, I have been crafting this concept of interviewing for years. At first, I was like you, going on interviews more times than I can remember- and under-whelmed with my performance. Sometimes my nerves got the best of me. That resulted in frustration. Other times, I blanked on answers. Why? Because I wasn't really prepared. So, I decided to be more reflective on what I actually brought to the table. Since then, I have been afforded the opportunity to sit on the other side of the table, as coach, mentor and interviewer. All those situations led me to create this book for you. Having a degree in Behavioral Science helped me to link behavior, aptitude and proficiencies. I will share this with you in three ways throughout this book.

1. I will coach you to self-reflect, a key skill in uncovering your every move during the interview process.

2. Acronyms, such as LEANBACK™ and SCAN™ will become familiar terminology to aid in self-discovery around your proficiencies and how to best represent them verbally in a polished way.

3. Sensory application. We will utilize three of the five senses; sight, touch and hearing to practice, practice, practice and create a foundation to verbalize your story.

But wait, before we get started, I feel the need to call out two fun ways to remember all of your awesomeness. As you uncover your strengths, you will want to find alternate ways to remember it all. Two techniques I have found useful are chunking and mnemonics.

Chunking is the ability to group information, making it easier to remember. For example, memorize these numbers: (not an actual number): 8881098621. Now, chunk it and see if it's easier to remember. 888–109–8621. By grouping or chunking, you essentially break down the unfamiliar, making it easier to remember.

When you utilize mnemonic technique, you are using association, imagery and even song to increase your memory. I remember when I was back in graduate school, I was about to take a Statistics test. I needed to do well. I used imagery! I assigned the names of friends and family to each study topic. As I took the test, their image appeared, and I was able to recall the needed information. It worked like a champ!

My method has been years in the making. I am excited to finally share it with you. In preparation I, too, have been systematic, strategic and seamless in my approach to cultivating this handbook so that you feel purposeful and proactive in getting that job. My goal with this handbook is to keep it simple yet packed with important points of reflection to raise your self-awareness and create a best-in-brand you!

We will go through the entire interview process. But, first, we will start with you. Chapter 1 will allow you to take a retrospective look at yourself. We will peel the onion away, layer by layer, so that you are fully aware of your conscious and subconscious actions and behaviors. Once you gain awareness regarding your behavior, Chapter 2 will teach you not only how to research a potential employment opportunity, but will start to formulate your preparation for understanding what a given employer is looking for.

Chapter 3 will bring us to our first acronym, LEANBACK™. Yes, it is an acronym AND title of my book. I just love the term *Lean Back* for so many reasons, first and foremost, for posturing, to help you visualize sitting back in your chair, commanding the attention of potential interviewers. I also love the name because it exudes confidence. And finally because everything you need to know about yourself, for your interview, will be found in this one acronym, LEANBACK. Chapter 4 will basically give you the keys to your kingdom. It is here that you will come to learn about my second acronym, SCAN™. This chapter is crucial in teaching you how to share a compelling story and ultimately maintain your interviewers' attention through the entire interview.

Chapter 5 will assist you in creating that virtual image through your resume, cover letter and other documents that will help you stand out against your competition. This will allow you to confidently *lean back* with the full package, and leave nothing in question.

Chapter 6 is the moment you've been waiting for. The interview! After reading this book, you will certainly be ready to *lean back* with your head held high. But, just to be sure there are no surprises, I have included an array of pearls to keep top of mind when you land that big day.

And, finishing out with Chapter 7 is all about the afterglow! What you do after the interview will demonstrate not only your follow through and attention to detail but will also show your resolve to keep your momentum focused, post interview.

So *Lean Back*, grab a pen and paper or your iPad/computer and get ready for a world of possibilities. The end result will yield a positive, poised, confident and prepared "you".

Leaning back in your chair, focused, purposeful and eager to share why YOU are the right person for the job will become your *modus operandi*!

CONTENTS

CHAPTER 1:

Reflection is a Life Skill

The best way to start the prep work on this core topic is to reflect on a time when previous interviews did not result in a job. Maybe you are thinking, *Go back to that devastating time in my life? Heck, no!* Why would I? To that I say comparison is a useful tool.

We have all had that moment in time when a previous interview resulted in not getting a much-wanted job or internship. When a given conversation went sideways and led to a difficult-to-understand rejection! Did you ever leave wondering what went wrong?

The interviewing process can be grueling and overwhelming. I feel your pain! I've been there as well. Sometimes our nerves get the best of us, causing a lack of true representation of our qualifications. These questions and thoughts will become clear as you read through my book.

I am a big believer in rejection being a good thing. If you are willing to own the opportunity! If you are willing to better yourself by reflecting on the "why" behind not getting that job!

Admittedly, it is a fact of life. A blow to the ego! But it will be another bit of self-help if you look it in the face and learn from it.

I'm here to tell you, I've been there! Done that! While not a good feeling, rejection… if looked at introspectively…. Will open the possibilities of self-awareness! Together, self-reflection and research will act as a "key in your interview ignition," and that will lead to more positive results. Important?

Very! Let me repeat: together, self-reflection and research will act as the "key in your interview ignition," and that will lead to more positive results.

Let's take some time to focus on self-reflection and research. "Self-Reflection" by definition is careful thought about something. With a Behavioral Science background, I feel the need to kick that up a bit. To me, reflection gives you the ability to examine your own conscious feelings and thoughts. It is an ability to look introspectively and to understand more about your essence and purpose in life. Not only is self-reflection an important skill for the job hunt, it is an added benefit, when done consistently, the golden key to a happier, more fulfilled life.

If you are wondering how to self-reflect, the answer is not complicated. It takes time, effort and the willingness to be honest with yourself to effectively learn from a given experience. I will share with you six ways to self-reflect. As you read through these six steps, look at the information with a two-pronged approach. Ask yourself these questions:

- What will I learn from a past experience?
- What will I learn about my behavior?

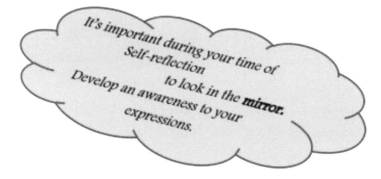

It's important during your time of
Self-reflection
to look in the mirror.
Develop an awareness to your
expressions.

How to self-reflect in 6 easy steps:

1. **Schedule time:** You and your thoughts are important! It is critical to block time on your calendar to create, a sense of accountability. You needn't block hours of time. In the beginning, set aside 15 minutes

for yourself. By doing this you will come to see a behavioral shift from reactive behavior to responsive behavior.

2. **Stay focused**: Have you ever wondered about the number of thoughts go through your mind in a given period of time? Experts report your mind has up to 60-80,000 thoughts per day.

   Drilling down more specifically, that would equate to approximately 3,000 thoughts per hour, 50 thoughts per minute. Lots of traffic in that mind of yours! Talk about distraction! So, when your mind starts wandering… STOP! Your short time of self-reflection should be purposeful and selfishly introspective.

3. **Observe:** "Be a spectator to your thinking." Take a listen to your cerebral audio and reflect on dialogue of past interviews. Allow yourself to be open and vulnerable to self-critique and pay attention to your body language as well. Your body language gives a nonverbal image to your mental psyche. Confidence, competence, negativity, insecurity, arrogance and even intimidation can be viewed through the skilled interviewer's lens. Observing your past interview conversations and how you were poised with body language will become an integral part of how you move forward with the next interview.

   I had one interviewee who constantly shook his leg during the interview. This distraction pulled my attention away from content and answers. Something as simple as a knee jerk can become the difference between nailing and not nailing that new job. Distraction happens to anyone. Always, it is a negative. Another interviewee never looked me in the eye. These aspects on body language can be misconstrued if you are not aware of it.

From the minute you step into the interview, it is important to have a keen awareness of your body's subconscious movements. Understand how they project your body's unique language.

Then, take control! Make your body movements work *for* you… not against you! Keep it all in P.E.R.S.P.E.C.T.I.V.E™. This key word and acronym will house everything you need to know about body language and other potential interviewing hazards.

P.E.R.S.P.E.C.T.I.V.E…Good word, don't ya think?

Here's what it stands for:

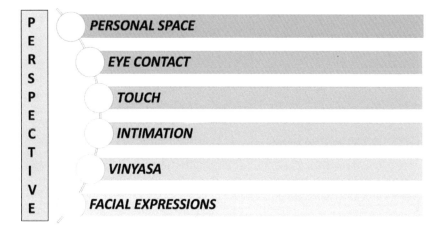

P	PERSONAL SPACE
E	
R	EYE CONTACT
S	
P	TOUCH
E	
C	INTIMATION
T	
I	VINYASA
V	
E	FACIAL EXPRESSIONS

Personal Space- (Represents the letters PERSP, in the acronym PERSPECTIVE™): We've all had friends who get so physically close to us that talking to them becomes uncomfortable due to the lack of distance and, maybe, they also need a breath mint. *Am I right?*

If you are so close to someone that you can actually smell their breath, especially in an interview, you may want to be mindful of their personal space. Personal Space is a comfort zone; within its confines, we may feel either secure or threatened by another individual, if distancing protocols are not observed.

For the purpose of interviewing, it is important to stay within the "personal zone" of 1.5-4 feet, 0.5-1.5m. This distance—- about an arm's length—- allows for direct conversation. Also, be mindful of the "intimate zone" (<1.5 feet, <0.5m.) If during an interview, you step into this zone—- which is shorter than your forearm—- it can be viewed as a power play or as threatening to the person, with whom you are conversing. Save this zone for your relationships and stand back!

Eye Contact- (Represents the letters EC in the acronym: PERSPECTIVE™): You've heard the saying, "Your eyes are the window to your soul." Believe it or not, your eyes do play a big role during the interviewing process. If you are not aware of the P.E.R.S.P.E.C.T.I.V.E™ pitfalls, you may, inadvertently, give the wrong impression!

Looking down at your feet, glancing at the sky, blinking excessively, etc., demonstrates a lack of confidence and honesty. Yet direct eye contact—- without staring—- will yield a confident, honest and well-mannered you.

And don't forget what I call "ocular expression!" It is important to show interest during the interview.

Without going into the anatomy and physiology of the eyes, it is a known fact your pupils dilate when you are passionate and/or interested about something. This physical reaction kicks in adrenaline which, to me, creates a sparkle in the eyes, and allows the interviewer to see your true interest in a given topic.

Touch- (Represents the letter T in the acronym: PERSPECTIVE™): Let's take a minute to talk about the handshake!

If there is anything you remember from my book, please remember this: a firm handshake opens the door to a world of possibilities. When I say firm, you do not want to give a handshake that leaves that person on his or her knees! Alternatively, a weak handshake (a.k.a. the fish shake) may leave the recipient of your grip wondering if you have had a local anesthetic injected, into your hand!

So, start off the interview with a professional handshake. Extend your right hand, give a firm grip and be mindful of your eye contact and serve it up with a smile! Okay?

Moving on to the subject of fidgety touch! This includes rubbing your thighs when answering a question, playing with a pen or the ever-popular rub of the nose, tweak of the neck and running your hands through your hair. They should be reserved for when you are at the gym.

Intimation- (Represents the letter I in the acronym: in PERSPECTIVE™): This is a fancy way of talking about our gestures, and it is another means of making something known in an indirect way. Therefore, it is import-ant to reflect, to gain a sense of awareness about how you use your hands, during conversations.

If you find you are entering a mime contest by using your hands to tell a story... sit on them! I'm kidding, but you do understand where I am going with this... yes? Excessive gestures, such as constantly nodding the head, jiggling keys in a pocket, hand movements or tapping your fingers on the table can be extremely distracting, and will take away from the message you are trying to convey.

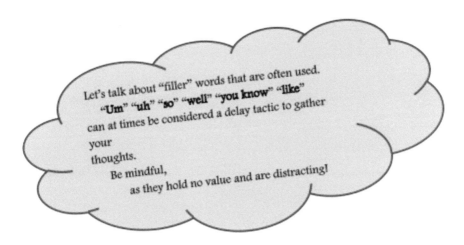

Let's talk about "filler" words that are often used.
"**Um**" "**uh**" "**so**" "**well**" "**you know**" "**like**"
can at times be considered a delay tactic to gather your
thoughts.
Be mindful,
as they hold no value and are distracting!

Vinyasa- (Represents the letter V in the acronym: PERSPECTIVE™): I thought it would be nice to incorporate a yoga term, by using the word Vinyasa. For those of you who have never taken a yoga class, allow me to give you a very brief peek into that lifestyle. (And, as a sidebar of conversation, I would truly encourage you to take a class or two. Talk about mind and body serenity. Of course, you should check with your doctor first).

Vinyasa is a method of yoga during which movements form a flowing sequence in coordination with your breathing. Ultimately, it allows you to develop a Mind Strong Body Strong mentality. I used the word Vinyasa, on purpose. It should open your thinking with regards to posture when interviewing. Sitting tall in your seat with hands on lap, feet planted on the floor, all while taking in consistent breaths, should be you state of Vinyasa. You will appear professional, polished and knowledgeable and will radiate confidence. Slouching and crossing your arms will yield a less than confident you.

Facial Expressions- (Represents the letter E in the acronym: PERSPECTIVE™): What is the best way to convey confidence via a facial expression? I bet you nailed it! It's your smile!

Did you know it takes approximately 17 muscles to create your smile and, approximately, 43 muscles to make you frown? Crazy, right! So, turn that frown upside down. Let's light up the interviewing room with your pearly whites, and take a closer look at why facial expressions, by definition, are a great form of non-verbal communication?

The answer? They talk to you with silent emotion. Don't be fooled! Not everyone has a poker player's face: not every face conceals emotion. Some inadvertently expose feelings of anger, contempt, disgust, fear, happiness, sadness and surprise.

Truth be told, I feel facial expressions are a universal language and can connect you in ways you never thought of. Whether you are sitting on the hot seat during an interview or chatting with friends, if you are conversing with someone who is not engaged, you will be hit with a blank stare.

Not good!

Engagement is key! Upon arrival at the interview, its game on! A firm handshake, good eye contact and that effervescent smile will open the doors to a confident, non-verbal presence. Okay? Aside from the magnetic smile, one must be mindful of the forehead and eyes. Furrowing your brow will make you look angry and/or or confused. Try your best to relax the procerus muscle, in your forehead to keep your face vibrant.

In closing, this question must be addressed. How should you look when engaged in a conversation during the all-important interview?

Communicate with your eyes! Look alert, keep that magnetic eye contact and blink every so often.

When I was interviewing, I always thought of a song, written by Chauncey Olcott & George Graff, Jr.! "When Irish Eyes Are Smiling!" In true form to the lyrics, "When Irish eyes are smiling sure, they steal your heart away," I always thought I would have a better interview outcome if I emulated those words. Usually, I did!

So, you can see that body language when viewed through the lens of the acronym P.E.R.S.P.E.C.T.I.V.E.™ is a concept to keep top of mind as you self-reflect.

Let's continue to explore other ways to self-reflect:

4. **Verbal acumen:** This is another important tool associated with self-reflection. I have used the following two words together on purpose; verbal + acumen= refined you!

    Ok, let's look at this!

    Acumen is all about being sharp, intuitive, understanding and intelligent. When your words resonate with acumen, you come across as polished, professional and possessing a keen strategic mindset.

    Think about this as you self-reflect on the choice of words you have used, in former interviews. Were you reactive and superficial in your conversations? Did you feel you could have answered the questions differently? Come across in a more eloquent way? Well, no worries. You will learn how to peel away unwanted layers from the onion of "interview presence" in the coming chapters.

5. **Auditory reverberation:** So, let me ask a question: Do you listen or do you hear? Have you thought about that? This is by far a key element with self-reflection.

    Did you truly listen to the interviewer's question or as they were talking, were you thinking about what you were going to say? The study of reactive as opposed to responsive listening has always intrigued me. I use the phrase of "reactive listening" vs "responsive listening" to expand on this topic.

    Reactive listening, A skill most definitely worth reflecting on is often times, emotionally based, void of initiative, and a causative factor in why you would quickly answer the interviewer's questions, without reflection. This type of listening derails a strategic mindset, leaving you with a superficial, limited response. Often a reactive listener comes across as being defensive because there is no reflection on the questions being asked.

This type of listener tends to scratch at the surface and misses an opportunity to engage at a thoughtful level. Many times, when we fall into this type of listening pattern, it is because we are caught off guard, not prepared and we shoot from the hip.

Another reason for this type of response is when we are interviewing, we hear certain buzz words. Immediately, we begin to formulate an answer. Even before the interviewer finishes the question. The end result with this type of listening will yield a misrepresented you.

Responsive listening means you are engaged, paying attention and looking beyond what is being said or discussed. This listening pattern puts you into a cerebral space to intellectually and eloquently respond to a given question. Responsive listening enables one to Lean Back in the hot seat. Yes?

People who are prepared and confident with the depth and breadth of their given role tend to be responsive listeners. They listen to the question, reflect on it, and take a moment to represent their thinking with a detailed proactive response. So, when I talk about auditory reverberation remember this. You have two ears and one mouth. Always, always listen twice and speak once.

6. **Mental disposition:** My final thought as we close out the section on self-reflection is to look back from a helicopter view of your total mind, body and spirit. I am sure you will agree we constantly have conversations in our heads. More often than not, these conversations tend to drive us down a negative pathway. We often second guess ourselves and the answers we have provided.

    As you self-reflect, be mindful of inner conversation's you had with yourself. Were you too wordy? Did you totally negate your answer? Were you being too hard on yourself?

The goal of this book is to increase your self-awareness and self-preparedness and reduce the chance of your mental disposition getting the best of you.

Wow- Let's pause for a moment to focus on self-reflection. Everything I have shared with you should be a point of conscious thought when you *Lean Back* in that interview chair. The more time you set aside to understand your own physical and emotional behavior via self-reflection, the better chance you will have in commanding the interview.

Do you want a job or a career? Know the difference!

CHAPTER 2:

Understanding the "Why"

Hand in hand with self-reflection is a process that brings your ultimate presence into the room. A behind-the-scenes necessity that allows you to understand the *why* behind your pursuit for this particular job, and the *why* you believe the available position fits your abilities like a glove! It is called research. It is called putting on your "thinking cap" to learn what the job is about, what type of proficiencies are required and mentally checking off those that you possess! It is learning about the company, its goals, structure, management and culture to see if you would be a good fit. If it would allow your true personality to blossom so you could achieve full business potential and be a valuable asset for your potential employer!

I can recall countless interviews where the potential candidate would say- on purpose mind you- that they chose not to do any research because they wanted to have an open mind when the interviewer explained what the company was looking for.

Oh, and here's another fall-on-your-face answer that I've heard one too many times.

Tell me what you think the job is about, I ask. The response- a made-up idea of what they thought the job was about. Think about that people! If you do not understand the job description, either read up on it or just don't go for it! Period.

You are entering a sea of talented competition, and as I mentioned in the introduction, when you get a response from classified's cyberspace, you better make sure you fully understand what you are getting yourself into. And research!

Let's give a shout out to our quiet, intelligent and always dependable friend- Google.

Let this search engine be your starting point for company research. Use LinkedIn to gain insights about potential interviewers. And yes, you can read these profiles in private mode. While we are on the subject of LinkedIn, have you taken a look at your own network? Do any of your connections have friends who work for the company you are going for? If so, network, over-prepare and deliver.

I'd like to take a moment to share some of my research with you, specifically around the title of my book. I truly hope the title, *Lean Back*, caught you eye and is one of the reasons you are reading this book. I spent hours on that title. I was determined to give this book a name that would speak to the message I wanted to convey. And that was to aid in the development of interviewee confidence, poise, articulation and effervescence during what I call Judgement Day.

My title research boiled down to that one moment in time when you sit on the hot seat.

When it is just you and the interviewer or just you and the panel of interviewers! A time when you want to exude confidence, impress with your knowledge, and be a winner.

I chewed on my research. Digested what I needed. Your ability to *Lean Back* at this life-changing moment in time would symbolize the inner confidence earned through preparation, research and self-reflection. Hence the title, *Lean Back*.

In the following chapter you will also come to see that this title is not only a state of mind but an acronym that will help you understand the proficiencies needed to progress on the interview pathway.

Yet, the term, research, will have different meanings depending on where you are in your lifecycle of employment. This book, *Lean Back*, will represent each of you, whether you are a high school student looking for an internship, or a college graduate seeking an entry-level job.

Stay-at-home moms, dads or partners who are entering/reentering the workforce due to the change of career will find a mentor in my book. It all comes down to preparation and research.

I love the quote by Benjamin Franklin, "By failing to prepare, you are preparing to fail."

Whatever position you are sitting on, the first step of research is with the job description itself.

Whether you are new to the workforce or moving into a leadership role, it all starts at the job posting. Take a look at what the company is looking for in a candidate. You will always find, what I call "proficiencies" listed in the job description. We will discuss them fully in the following chapters.

Below, you will find two diagrams, labeled "The Green Zone" and "The Blue Zone."

These two zones will help you get started in researching and building your story. The "green zone" allows you to learn about the potential job and company. The "blue zone" will pull in the "why." Why you are the right person for the job!

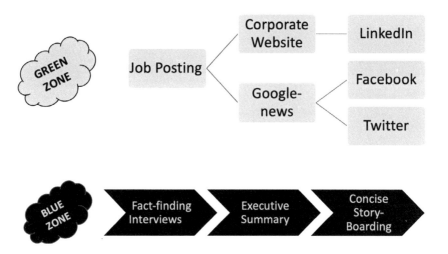

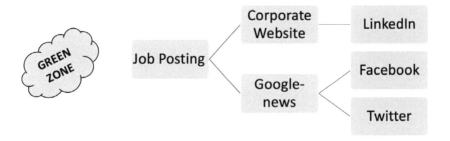

Job Postings

- Role description: Look for key words and phrases to incorporate in your resume and/or cover letter. Reading between the lines here will, to a degree, reveal the corporate culture. This sets expectations.

- Role responsibilities: This is where you look for alignment with your skillsets. You need to write these responsibilities from the job posting on a piece of paper. Then pair your accomplishments next to those that are relevant. Key insights and accomplishments should be on your resume and cover letter. The best way to accomplish this is to create a spreadsheet labeling your skillsets and the jobs' role responsibilities.

- Company description: The job posting will list a history of the company, what it stands for, its values and working culture. The age of the company, as well as whether it is national, international, regional, etc., will also be listed. If you are interested in job longevity, this is an important read. Yes, think long term. At some point in time, you may want to relocate. Therefore, it is important to get the full scope of the corporate history, culture and vision.

- Preferred minimum qualifications: This is where a crossroad occurs between our new recruits and savvy, experienced members of the workforce. In looking at minimum qualifications, it is important to have experience in what they are looking for.

For my new folks entering the workforce, you will want to start looking at "entry-level" positions. That should negate that experience question.

For experienced members of the workforce, you know this all too well and have accumulated extensive skillsets to meet many of the qualifications.

- Logistical intel: It contains: type of employment, location of the position, details on how to apply, name of contact person for questions, timeline of posting, and a description of the company.

Once you gain these insights from the job description, you will want to explore their website to understand their vision, long-term strategy and overall perspective on their culture.

Corporate Website:

May I say you just hit the lotto! Well, not really! However, by going on the corporate website you will have unlocked all you need to know and more about the company!

A company website can be a little overwhelming. Start by clicking on the "About Us" tab. This will give you a good history of the company, any awards won and their vision.

I would encourage you to learn their mission, understand their values and be able to talk to it fluently. It would be brilliant to take that information and tie it to a time that you have lived that value or a similar experience.

News and recent events will also be published on their site, read through them. Weave some of the storyline into your interview. It shows you have gone above and beyond in learning about your potential employer

It's also important to look at their product portfolio and services rendered. This will give you an understanding of what you will be working with.

The leadership team is important to view as well. Gain familiarity with who they are, the scope of their role and their respective visions.

LinkedIn:

LinkedIn is one of the top professional networking sites. If you are not on LinkedIn, you are missing out. Once you create a LinkedIn profile, make sure you keep it up to date. Use key buzzwords that will increase traffic to your page. Highlight key experiences, and be sure to be detailed around your current skillsets.

Add a profile picture and headline that highlights what you do. You can also use your headline to advertise your search for a job.

Network, network, network. Start with your friends, then look at their friends. Also follow companies to increase your visibility.

LinkedIn acts as a dual-pronged approach: one prong allows you to highlight who you are, the competencies/experiences you represent, and to get views from potential companies and recruiters. The other prong gives you the visibility to research the people you are going to interview with.

To browse profiles in private or semi-private mode, follow these steps:

- Click the "Me" icon at the top of the LinkedIn homepage.
- Select Settings & Privacy from the dropdown.
- Click on Visibility.
- Click on Profile Viewing Options.
- Select the mode you would like to browse in. You will have three options.
- Happy browsing.

Google/Google News:

In addition to LinkedIn, you can search Google if you know the interviewer's name. Look for anything you might have in common with these individuals.

Google the company's name to gain insight, including whether this company is legitimate.

Use Google news (news.google.com) to understand the publicity, stock price, expansions, awards given, etc., of the company.

Google will also provide any negative press the company has faced.

The more you know about a given company and the people you are going to interview with, the easier the conversation. This also shows the interviewer that you are "all-in" and invested in being a part of the organization.

Facebook and Twitter:

Utilize these social platforms as an additional resource to tap into the social side of the interviewer. You may find that you have similar interests. Weave them into your story during the interview.

Use the search bar on Facebook to look up the company. You will be amazed with what you find. You will see company groups, jobs offered, background to the company and people who liked the page. Search the names to see if you know anyone. If you do network!

Don't forget to look at the comments listed. Identify whether it is positive or negative feedback.

Use Facebook to search the company's pages to increase your knowledge around products, services, work-life balance etc.

Remember, they can't see you viewing their profile so search out where they went to school, previous employment history, and common interests.

Twitter reveals a realistic view to a company as well. So, explore. The more you know, the greater the advantage you will gain to nailing that position.

Continuing on with your research, we will now move into the "Blue Zone." The Blue Zone will allow you to take what you learned about the potential position and company and match it to your accomplishments and skills.

Until now you have been flying solo, exploring every angle to see if your accomplishments and skills are a good match for the job. Now, I introduce to you the opportunity to dig deeper. And that is through, what I call, fact-finding interviews.

Fact-finding Interviews:

This is an opportunity to get a first-hand perspective from a given employee that will give you great insight into a day in the life at that given company. This also allows you to ask some key questions. The answers will give you a well-rounded view of the position you are going for.

Once you dive in to your research, you will have a better understanding of the job at hand, the interviewer and company philosophy. You will then be able to ask insightful questions.

Reach out to your connections on LinkedIn. Set up time to talk. Here are a few questions you can ask:

- What do you like most about your work/company?
- What is the greatest challenge you face at work?
- How does your job affect your lifestyle?

Executive Summary:

Developing an executive summary will provide the interviewer an opportunity to understand your thought process from a behavioral, cognitive and social perspective.

Executive summaries highlight your resume yet will call out your forward thinking. Remember, your resume demonstrates past experiences. You will want to demonstrate a future focus. How you plan on achieving success in your new role. Sit tight! We will discuss the nuts and bolts of an Executive Summary in the coming chapters.

Concise Storytelling:

Concise Storytelling is a crucial catalyst in conveying your experiences during the interview. Keeping your story succinct will keep the attention of your interviewer.

As we work to develop your story, be mindful of my previous advice around self-reflection. You must understand how you normally converse with another individual to be an effective storyteller. Do you tend to go off on tangents? Use filler words like *umm*? Do you misrepresent your intentions? Perhaps, come across aggressive or angry? Do you see where I am going with this? I could go on about storytelling, but my point is to button it up. More words are not always a good thing.

How do you use the research you have so diligently worked at collecting and share this information without coming across aggressive, self-absorbed or even arrogant?

No worries, we will focus on creating a great story so that you will be able to *Lean Back* in your chair and highlight your accomplishments in a polished and gracious way. This will come in the upcoming chapters.

CHAPTER 3:

Breaking the Ceiling with my Proficiency Model; LEANBACK™

Proficiencies equal the sum of our experiences! Makes sense, right?

Past business capabilities, whether good or bad, bring about a story to be shared with your interviewer for they inadvertently spotlight various proficiencies you have either succeeded or failed at. Therefore, it is important to bring both success and failure to life at that critical moment in your search for employment.

You may be thinking, is Mo actually telling me to share my failures at an interview? The short answer is yes and no.

If you have never experienced failure, you have been living in your comfort zone, not taking risks or you have been in complete denial. Failure as well as success is an important part of your story. But what you will share with your interviewer is something I call proficiencies, the behavior *behind* a particular failure or success!

Before we proceed, let's get something out in the open: no one is perfect. Did you get that? No one, male or female, is a Mary Poppins protégé, practically perfect in every way. And that is a good thing! For it is in the true grit of failed attempts at success that our ability, to succeed, gets a jump start and pushes us closer to victory.

Plainly speaking, we learn from our mistakes. Practice *really* does make perfect!

Remember, wherever you are on the pendulum of employment, you do have a story, complete with proficiencies to tell at your interview. Whether you are a recent graduate, a returnee to the workforce or a current employee looking for that change of career or promotion, you will bring to your interview stories that will translate into, what I call, proficiencies.

By focusing on them you will gain a detailed understanding of how your experiences will be defined through the lens of my proficiency model: LEANBACK™.

This section will require your complete focus as well as your ability to effectively use the self-reflection tools discussed in previous chapters. Are you ready to acquire the ability to effectively sell yourself via a written story that will detail the proficiencies you bring to the table? Is that smile on your face, a yes?

Well, let's go! Game on! I am happy to introduce you to your newest best friend: my LEANBACK™ Proficiency Model.

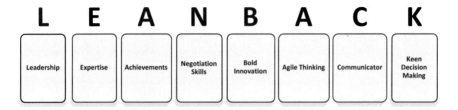

Leadership

I have always disliked reading books that provide the definition to a given topic by using merely the word itself, without giving any deep understanding of the concept. Confused? Me too! Here is an example; "The definition of leadership is the act of leading." Seriously?

Now, you may be starting out in the workforce and panic may be setting in because you have never held a leadership position. Don't worry! There are many ways to lead without being labeled a "leader/manager." Some terms come to mind such as, coach, teacher, taking a lead or co-lead for a project, school room parent or organization volunteer, etc.

Also, there are positions out there where people manage without formal authority. Basically, the implied boss is in a role that requires him/her to perform as a leader. Yet he/she is not the employee's direct report. Technically, the co-worker is not required to listen or obey.

This informal status requires the ability to raise a co-worker's knowledge around a task that needs to be done, bring him/her into the fold with value propositions and partner with him/her to get the job done. And then there are those who have stepped into leadership roles. All tend to possess a high level of social intelligence with an overarching belief in their people.

Leadership, a proficiency term, is described as being a mindset where one drives for results.

To best understand that concept, I compare the definition of leadership with the process required to shoot an arrow. The archer

- Makes a stand, assumes the shooting position and nocks the arrow
- Draws and anchors the bow
- Takes aim
- Releases the string and follows through

Got that? Okay, close your eyes. Visualize yourself as the archer. Now, open your eyes and cross-reference the definition of leadership with shooting an arrow.

To stand and assume the shooting position is the same thing as setting a fundamental goal for a given project.

Nocking the arrow is like delegating roles and responsibilities to achieve that goal/ project.

Making sense? Do you see how this comparison applies to your role as a leader?

Drawing and anchoring the bow would be equivalent to assessing the progress of the project.

Taking aim correlates in leadership to reviewing your project to ensure nothing is missing.

Releasing the string is simply setting a timeline to completion. And checking back to ensure the goal/ project has been accomplished is plain old-fashioned follow through.

All steps were necessary to shoot the arrow; all steps are important tools for a successful leader. Leadership, at any stage of employment, is all about inspiring and influencing. It is where you have the ability to foster an exchange of ideas and promote a vision that people will want to act on. It is about managing change, when you have remained positive, proactive and agile during times of uncertainty. It involves being open to feedback as well as being a good coach.

Examples of what a leader should not do to litter the business landscape? One particular story comes to mind. A former manager had to discuss a critical matter with an employee. Emotions ran high. The boss talked "at" the receiver. The conversation went sideways and shut down the lines of communication. The boss's ability to lead that person was compromised.

Words are so important. So is attitude! It takes time as well as a determined focus and resolve a situation to foster growth and learning.

Leaders tend to possess a high level of social intelligence with an overarching theme of being an ambassador of belief in their people. Leadership is a valued proficiency.

YOUR TURN: Reflect on a time where you have demonstrated this proficiency and write it down below:

_____

_____

_____

_____

_____

Expertise (Business, Professional and Technical)

There are many levels of expertise, but to me, expertise is taking a stand to push through the status quo.

Some people have a thirst for knowledge, some an intense interest in a given subject. As a result of this curiosity and/or interest, they inadvertently become experts on that subject. But, for the purpose of this book we will focus on business, professional and technical expertise. It is a totally different ballgame.

When you think of examples that will demonstrate your expertise in a given area, remember that this can talk to innate abilities and acquired skills honed over the years. Remember to speak eloquently on the given subject.

Pursuing a job requires the applicant to demonstrate expertise in a given area. This brings to life your ability to go above and beyond regardless of the topic. Whether you are a graduating student or a person re-entering the workforce, you have most likely gained some kind of proficiency in that arena.

If you are already in the workforce, your job has enabled or will enable you to grow in knowledge around verbalizing your understanding and accomplishments, with examples in expertise. Some examples of these questions are: What is your knowledge around a given subject? Are you able to assess trends, and or demonstrate how you remain current on a given subject?

One key callout I will make is this. You must demonstrate self-awareness when speaking as an "expert" during the interview. One could come across as a know-it-all and cause the interviewer to misinterpret your proficiency.

To avoid this situation, walk a fine line when sharing your level of expertise. Know your audience through the research you did for the interview. It's like a football game; go wide or deep, but know the playbook to efficiently run the conversation.

Business and professional expertise talk to your credibility, and to past experiences where you were able to elevate the co-worker learning curve. Technical expertise will round out your ability to be an effective problem solver. Many companies truly value and often rely on those with technical expertise. This type of knowledge empowers the company to develop further and be the best they can be.

Peeling the onion away to this concept of "expertise," let's look at some examples to give you a jumpstart to look within and realize you bring more to the table than you thought.

Examples of business expertise include, but are not limited to, problem solving, negotiating, team building, time management, project planning, etc. Professional expertise can speak to public speaking, showing initiative, conflict resolution, communication and meeting deadlines. And lastly, technical expertise can speak to data analysis, software proficiency, coding and programming and even social media management and marketing.

Having business, professional and technical expertise brings to light an inner confidence that allows you to *Lean Back* in sharing these stories.

YOUR TURN: Reflect on a time where you have demonstrated this proficiency and write it down below:

_____

_____

_____

_____

_____

Achievements

In my opinion, this proficiency is probably is the most important. If you haven't achieved anything prior to your interview, it's going to be an uphill battle to demonstrate your worth with a given job. With that said, achieving results is a simple term with a wide array of details encompassed within.

Let's be honest, your achievements bring into the spotlight many concepts: planning, execution, follow through and ultimately organizational savvy.

One cannot achieve without prepping. As the saying goes, "Fail to prepare, prepare to fail."

Now, don't get me wrong, achieving results can be met with a positive ending or a not so positive ending. Both are actually good because whether it worked or not, you have demonstrated the concept of learning, hard work, success and sometimes failure. In hindsight, what did you learn from a successful result and equally what did you learn from a failed result?

You see, interviewers will look to uncover something called resilience. Do you adapt well in the face of adversity? Do you take responsibility for your actions? Do you give up? Do you fail to reflect on what you could have done differently?

Remember, failure is the mother of invention. So when you look at achieving results, think of a time when you thought outside the box to solve a problem or when you needed to be flexible with a project.

Timelines come into play here as well. Did you meet your deadline? Were you ahead of schedule or behind? All of which tells a story about you, your character and integrity. Again, this proficiency is, to me, very important to reflect on.

Your failures are equally as important as your successes. Think about some experiences in your life where you had to plan, execute, and sometimes pivot in a new direction to deliver.

Before I close out this proficiency, one concept I need to elaborate on is the term, "organizational savvy." This concept is different than being organized in your approach to tackling a given project. Yes, you must be organized from a mental and physical perspective to reduce stress and increase your efficiency by making schedules, being proactive and focused with you time, etc. But organizational savvy talks to the mindset you develop to navigate organizational politics.

Did you know how to operate to get things done while in school or at a previous job? Are you savvy about the meaning of acting on what's written as well as reading between the lines to understand the intent behind what is not written?

Organizational savvy is an acquired skill. It can set you apart from the best-of-the-rest. How? By affording you the hyper awareness of the "why."

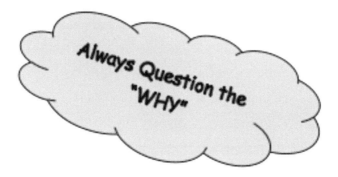

Learn as much as you can about the internal mechanics of your organization. Focus on what motivates them. Be an active participant by being all-in.

YOUR TURN: Reflect on a time where you have demonstrated this proficiency and write it down below:

_____

_____

_____

_____

_____

Negotiation Skills

A negotiation is a purposeful dialogue with another individual or a group of people. The focus is on content and outcome with an undercurrent of resolving conflict or differences in order to achieve a desired outcome.

The proficiency of negotiation skills aligns in a parallel universe to teamwork and collaboration. This concept should stretch your thinking to uncover areas where you have demonstrated a collaborative spirit when on a team or when you needed to have ready the ability to negotiate your stance for a desired outcome! Simply stated, this involves dialoging on the features and benefits of a given situation and having the ability to create a paradigm shift for a desired outcome.

Most interviewers will strive to uncover how you operate within a group setting via precise questioning. Are you a team player or is it an "all about me show?" What position do you play in team dynamics? Do you take the lead? Focus on getting your point across? Are you able to lead individuals? To pull them together in a safe arena to voice their opinions or do you sit back and go with the flow? Do you embrace the diversity of the team to include alternate points of view?

Answers to these questions are critical to the success of your interview. Use tools learned in previous chapters. Chew on words. Digest sentences. Understand their application to your situation before you speak.

Your answers will enable the interviewer to gain insight into your ability and/or agility to embrace different approaches in a non-territorial way.

Another aspect to call out is a team dynamic that went sideways. Suppose you were a member of an aggressive adversarial team? And they acted up? The opposing team called them out! Negotiations hit the wall! Failure was ready to take a bow!

How would you handle this? These are aspects that need to be captured for your story.

YOUR TURN: Reflect on a time where you have demonstrated this proficiency and write it down below:

_____

_____

_____

_____

_____

Bold Innovation

Here's a shout out to my readers! You don't need to be a rocket scientist to innovate. And you don't need a patent attorney to own this proficiency. This innate as well as developed trait works hand in hand with a high level of self-awareness. When stretched, developed and honed to perfection from a business perspective it will yield you many accolades for thinking out of the box.

The goal of innovation is to increase efficiency. And it doesn't have to be something you can touch! Look around you. Put on your thinking cap!

How can you improve the status quo? Will changing a rule to increase productivity or finding an easier way to sell a product help? Creating a new process of working differently? Inventing something that will benefit a larger audience?

Let me share one example of innovation from my experience. Whiles working with a former sales team, I wanted to bring them together to increase their knowledge around certain aspects of the job. So, I created a program called "Access Momentum." (The mo in momentum was a play on my nick-name, Mo.) After stating goals and expectations, my team strategized and collectively provided input. I created T-shirts to give out whenever a member of the team demonstrated proficiency and/or expertise in a given area.

My innovation in creating this award and making it fun to learn was a great success. It sparked enthusiasm, raised team spirit and the team's increased level of product knowledge resulted in higher sales, happier customers and, everyone wanting a T-shirt!

Since this segment is about innovation, I am, here to tell you the more you speak "of" something instead of talking "to" something the more you are getting under the hood of a given topic. You are owning that topic with full understanding. You are all-in!

When you speak "to" something, it's more of a superficial conversation, one with no meat to the content. But, when you speak "of" something, you should be able to teach anyone regardless of the person's level of sophistication. And that's where innovation comes into play! If you can look into something, chances are you can see what's working, what's not working, where the gaps are, etc.

This is what I shout from the mountaintop tops! What I tell my kids all the time! When you speak "of" something, you must study, investigate and understand it. Bluffs won't do. You must know what you are talking about. Know the product, rule and/or situation! So you can defend your position's negatives, if required.

Store every scintilla of information in a lockbox, in the deepest recesses, of your brain. Bring it forth with confidence. And win the day!

Let's have some fun! What have you done differently to increase the process or service or even create a product to meet unmet needs, which in turn increased the effectiveness of your particular situation?

YOUR TURN: Reflect on a time where you have demonstrated this proficiency and write it down below:

_____

_____

_____

_____

_____

Agile Thinking

Well, that is a mouthful! Let's break this down. Agile is the ability to transition well. Having a flexible mindset, one can pivot easily to changes that occur in the workplace. When you are agile, you adapt easily. You tend to have a lower level of frustration. Why? You have the ability to shift your mindset so as to create a positive outcome.

Thinking strategically is a form of forward thinking to an internal dialogue around an idea. A belief and/or thought that creates a broad impact by creating a linkage to strategies, tactics for increased awareness and ultimately a successful outcome.

Let me ask you a question. Are you a one-woman/ one-man show, doing everything on your own? Do you position yourself like Atlas? Carrying the weight of the world on your shoulders? Well, remember Atlas! A leader for the Titans, was punished at the end of the Titanomachy to eternally hold up the heaven on the western edge of the world and eventually turned to stone. Not a good outcome for a brilliant leader!

My point! The more you look globally at a given situation, the more you realize that you need help not only to get the job done, but also to increase creative concepts to achieve abundant success.

To me, Strategic Agility links nicely with innovation. Simply put, having strategic agility will lead you down a pathway of looking at the outcome of what you are trying to achieve and then asking yourself "how." How can I best achieve that outcome? Who do I need to pull on to my team to increase the level of expertise?

By having that wherewithal mindset, you are demonstrating strategic agility. With that said, it's your turn to think of a time that you had to be flexible in your thinking. When you had to pull other thought leaders in to either raise awareness to a complex matter or create a successful outcome to a given project.

YOUR TURN: Reflect on a time where you have demonstrated this proficiency and write it down below:

_____

_____

_____

_____

_____

Communicator

Communication is such a simple term. People communicate all the time. But make no mistake. This proficiency takes time to master. It's like learning to swim. The more practice you take with your strokes, the better a swimmer you will be. Same goes for communication! It is not all about talking, it is about engaging.

Interestingly enough, effective communicators are brilliant listeners. The reason we have two ears and one mouth is because we are supposed to listen twice and speak once. When we communicate, we exchange our ideas, thoughts, opinions, facts, etc. to another individual, group or organization.

Some books speak to additional types of communication but, in my opinion, there are only four:

- Visual,

- Written

- Non-Verbal,

- Verbal.

Having a degree in Behavioral Science, I am going to start the conversation with a look at Visual communication.

Have you ever had a conversation with someone who constantly looks at his/her phone? They need a lesson in visual communication! Not only is that rude, it limits engagement.

Visual communication is twofold. It can be viewed, no pun intended, as a communication tool with charts, images, slides, etc., to share a thought as well as using those eyes of yours to focus on that person and show them you are listening.

Written communication has exploded with the advent of technology. It conveys vital information via text, email, letters, tests, resumes, etc.

Non-verbal communication is like entering one of those silent parties. It is communication without using the spoken language. Body language, facial expressions, gestures, all can either get you into a lot of trouble or enhance your connection with another.

And finally there is verbal communication, he ability to express yourself with sounds and words! OK, we have literally just touched the surface on communication. I could write for hours on this proficiency, but I think you get the gist of what it's all about. Now, some interviewers will not only look to see how you communicate but they may ask you to talk about it. Not only are they looking for content here, but they are also looking to see if what you say is genuine and authentic and if are you able to tailor your communication style to fit different audiences. This proficiency can pull in some strategic agility to flex your thinking as well.

YOUR TURN: Reflect on a time where you have demonstrated this proficiency and write it down below:

_____

_____

_____

_____

_____

Keen Decision Making

Keen decision making is the ability to look at multiple scenarios, analyze each one, and select the best possible choice. This proficiency requires critical thinking to ensure the implications of that decision are thoroughly considered. Critical thinking is the ability to *Lean Back* and question. To uncover additional details and not simply accept the information put in front of you!

Think of decision-making as a ladder to success. Step one: Uncover the problem. Step two: Gather all information. Step three: Look at alternatives. Step four: Evaluate and analyze the evidence. Step five: Take action. Step six: Assess your decision and the outcome.

Interviewers will be looking to see your problem-solving aptitude here via your response. This will be conveyed via formal and/or informal examples. We make decisions every day. They can be simple or highly competitive. You need to self-reflect to look at the outcome of any given decision.

What process did you follow to make a decision? Have you ever had to make a difficult decision that was unpopular? Have you had the opportunity to be in authority, to make decisions? What was the outcome? Again, I must remind you, outcomes may be positive or negative. Both come with a wide array of learning. The insight the interviewer is looking for is what you did *with* the outcome.

YOUR TURN: Reflect on a time where you have demonstrated this proficiency and write it down below:

_____

_____

_____

_____

_____

We have completed a journey of self-reflection, looking at and exposing our very own proficiencies, while utilizing my analogy of LEANBACK™. I hope you have taken the time to write down examples of how you have demonstrated each of the proficiencies listed. The more you peel away the onion to reveal who you are and how you operate, the better you will represent yourself in a poised and confident manner.

One of the reasons I wrote this book was to alleviate the nervous energy that comes with interviewing, by allowing you to *Lean Back* and tell your story.

One key callout out I will also share is that you may not be required to address every proficiency during your interview. The interviewer may be looking for three of these proficiencies or five. Regardless, the better you know your story, the easier your interview will be.

The next chapter will pull this all together. You will be able to share, with purpose, who you are and what you bring to that potential job.

CHAPTER 4

Let's SCAN™ Your Proficiencies.

My SCAN™ method will keep your interviewer's attention because you are giving the solution up front

You are in the home stretch. The previous chapter should have taken you a substantial amount of time to reflect on, research and capture major strengths starring you! Be mindful, employers will test you to see if you can handle the job.

If you have not completed work on your LEANBACK™ proficiencies, then go back. Review that chapter. You will need its content for this chapter. Trust me! The more you are able to speak eloquently about yourself, the easier the interview will be. The preparation and understanding you will bring to it will serve you well.

This following chapter will also require your input, thoughts and tons of facts. I truly believe the outcome of this pre-work will yield a confident you who is ready to *Lean Back* and tackle any type of interview.

So, how will this happen, you ask? Simply stated, you will take all the work you just completed in the last chapter and organize your thoughts into a succinct story via my personally designed system I call SCAN™.

SCAN™ will allow you to streamline your story, increase focus on key points to convey during your interview and allow your mind to chunk the sections to assist you in recalling a given proficiency from my LEANBACK™ concept. Utilizing SCAN™, you will command attention during the interview!

Before we begin to SCAN™ your proficiencies, I want to call out the fact that interviewing is a lot like therapy. It truly is all about YOU! I know, you are thinking it's really up to the interviewer to see if you are a good fit for their organization. But, that's not necessarily the whole truth. You are interviewing them as much as they are interviewing you. Trust me when I say that if you follow my instructions, you will be able to answer any question the interviewer throws at you. And as an added benefit, you will have developed an insightful awareness that will enable you to see if that company is a good fit for you.

So, when approaching this thing called an interview, be ready to say, "What else can I share with you to help you understand why I'm a good fit for this job?"

Let's get ready to SCAN™ your proficiencies. Create a succinct story that melds with each LEANBACK™ proficiency. Let's face it, we live in a world of immediate gratification. The last thing an interviewer wants to listen to is someone who goes off on tangents, utilizes too many filler words and doesn't get to the point in an abbreviated amount of time. Being succinct and solutions-oriented is the key in sharing your story because, as I mentioned earlier, you want to keep the attention of your interviewer and they want to hear impact up front. Hence, I created the SCAN™ concept where you share the solution up front. Then you share how you attained your goal and why it was important.

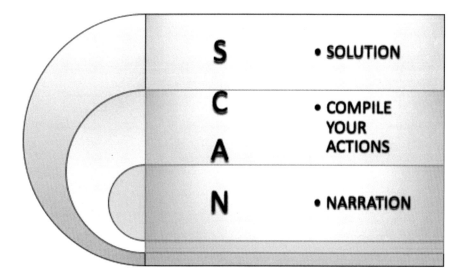

The goal is to take what you learned from previous chapters such as what's involved in the acronym PERSPECTIVE™. This will enable you to be proactive in your conversation. Verbal acumen partnered with confidence and an upbeat mental disposition will deliver profound yet concise answers to any interviewer's questions.

Actually, SCAN™ can be a fun exercise. But only if you bring to the table a willingness to give full exposure to your actions! The devil is in the details. Yet, you must be concise when verbalizing your accomplishments. So, let's begin to SCAN™ our proficiencies by understanding what I mean by that acronym.

The Solution "S"

What has been done to resolve a situation? This is where you set the stage to answer all "can you" questions. The **solution** gives you the opportunity to freeze a specific moment in time in an overarching way. So, when you review LEAN BACK™ proficiencies, pick the one where you have described a specific event that took place within the confines of that given proficiency. Hopefully, you have listed an example next to every LEANBACK™ proficiency. Depending on where you are in the employment paradigm, you may have limited or extensive examples. Either way, this is where you grab your interviewer with the overarching lens of a given story. How?

Don't be too wordy. And don't try to guess what proficiency the interviewer is looking for. Never second-guess! Never say, "I believe you are asking a question on decision-making. "That is a rabbit hole you do not want to go down. You are not there to play guessing games. You are there to share your story, period! The interviewer will see what you bring to the table through your examples.

The better you know your stories the better you will be able to bring your interviewer on a journey that highlights your successes. So, when an interviewer asks you to describe a time or share an example of… be gracious. Acknowledge him/her by saying, "Great question! Or, "I'd love to share an example of when I demonstrated that given question." Then you say, "Here's what was done." Give the solution in a succinct way. Then move into how it was done.

Compile Your Actions "CA": How It Was Done!

Earlier I said, "The devil is in the details." Remember? Well, this is the time you will convey the steps you took to address that given situation. "What was the task at hand?" "How did you accomplish it?" And "What was your responsibility and/or role with this situation?" "Did you need to pull other people in to gain additional insight?" "Did you need to create a document, spreadsheet, survey, etc. to align on priorities of that given example?"

While you are pulling your examples together it is imperative to be mindful of how many times you utilize the word "I". When you use the word, "I," the interviewer may assume you are not a collaborator. As you are practicing, make a mental callout to the number of times "I" is mentioned. You can simply change it to "we."

Are you starting to see the value in prepping for an interview?

Take a look at one of the proficiencies you wrote down in the previous chapter. Tease out the detailed actions of that situation. I encourage you to be very detailed here and write everything down. Once that is done, your job is to analyze the pertinent points. Write them down without being too wordy.

Narration "N"

Why it was done! Simply put, this is the icing on the cake. Highlighting your solution by compiling your actions will result in your genuine narration around why it was important and the impact it made. "What was the end result to this given situation?" "Did it work out successfully?" "Did you meet a time commitment?" The main goal here is to bring to life the positive impact you made. It is also an opportunity to share feedback you received from your colleagues, management, etc. Another key point. Every SCAN™ you present should be met with a positive result.

Now, I am going to speak out of both sides of my mouth. It is also important to convey when a given SCAN™ did not meet with good results. What an interviewer wants to see here is how did you handle this situation?

Did you get frustrated and just give up? Did you play the blame game? Or did you take ownership and learn from that experience?

Both sides of this SCAN™ uncover how you handle both success and failure. I'll go out on a limb here and say if you feel you haven't experienced failure, then you are either in denial or have lived in your comfort zone for way too long. Perfection is overrated. It is in the moments of failure that we learn and grow. Failure breeds pressure to overcome the status quo.

I love this example and have shared it with my kids one too many times. Carbon without pressure is just carbon. But carbon under pressure will yield diamonds. Now, I'm not a science expert but I think you understand where I'm going with this. Pressure and failure will yield a beautiful output if you just *lean back* to it.

Below, you will find space to capture your SCAN™ on each of the LEANBACK™ proficiencies. This is a good time to talk about the nervous energy one experiences at a given interview. It can be debilitating. It can turn your interview sideways.

By following the methods in this book, by knowing your story and verbalizing it over and over before your interview, you will be saying, "Goodbye, nervousness! Hello, confidence!"

I have used my method and have been met with great success. But at the end of the day, it's a lot to remember. Think about it! There are a multitude of facts to be delivered to the interviewer in a short period of time. Preparation and follow-through are prime, but you might need another tool in your toolbox.

I'd like you to think about ways to increase your bandwidth of memory.

As mentioned in Chapter 1, utilize chunking and mnemonics to aid in retention. Take some time to collect your thoughts. Put pen to paper. SCAN™ your proficiencies on the following workshop page.

Give it a try! It can't hurt, and it will help!

NARRATION

**COMPILE
ACTIONS**

SOLUTION

LEADERSHIP

SOLUTION:

_____
_____
_____
_____

COMPILE ACTIONS:

_____
_____
_____
_____
_____
_____
_____
_____
_____

NARRATION:

_____

_____

_____

_____

_____

_____

EXPERTISE (BUSINESS, TECHNICAL)

SOLUTION:

_____

_____

_____

_____

COMPILE ACTIONS:

_____

_____

_____

_____

_____

_____

_____

_____

_____

NARRATION:

_____

_____

_____

_____

_____

_____

ACHIEVEMENTS

SOLUTION:

_____

_____

_____

_____

COMPILE ACTIONS:

_____

_____

_____

_____

_____

_____

_____

_____

_____

NARRATION:

_____

_____

_____

_____

_____

_____

NEGOTIATION SKILLS

SOLUTION:

_____

_____

_____

_____

COMPILE ACTIONS:

_____

_____

_____

_____

_____

_____

_____

NARRATION:

_____

_____

_____

_____

_____

BOLD INNOVATION

SOLUTION:

_____

_____

_____

_____

COMPILE ACTIONS:

_____

_____

_____

_____

_____

_____

_____

_____

NARRATION:

_____

_____

_____

_____

_____

_____

AGILE THINKING

SOLUTION:

_____

_____

_____

_____

COMPILE ACTIONS:

_____

_____

_____

_____

_____

_____

_____

_____

NARRATION:

_____

_____

_____

_____

_____

_____

COMMUNICATOR

SOLUTION:

_____

_____

_____

_____

COMPILE ACTIONS:

_____

_____

_____

_____

_____

_____

_____

_____

NARRATION:

_____

_____

_____

_____

_____

_____

KEEN DECISION-MAKING

SOLUTION:

_____

_____

_____

_____

COMPILE ACTIONS:

_____

_____

_____

_____

_____

_____

_____

_____

NARRATION:

_____

_____

_____

_____

_____

_____

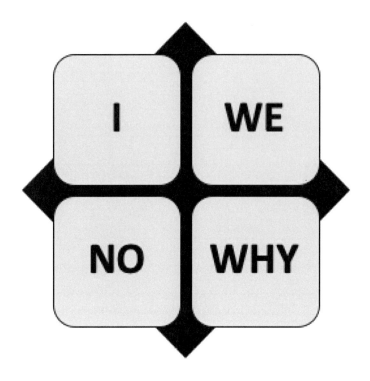

As you take time to reflect on the SCAN™ of each LEANBACK™ proficiency, I want you to highlight any SCAN™ that speaks to the above four quadrants, "I", "We," "No" and "Why."

Interviewers will generally ask questions that speak to each of the quadrants. For example:

- Can you tell me about a time where you had a number of conflicting demands on you time? How did you proceed and what was the outcome? (Talks to **"I."**)

- Describe a time when you had to pull together and foster cooperation between different team members? (Talks to **"We."**)

- Tell me about a time when you had to deal with a serious problem raised by a dissatisfied client? What did you do? (Speaks to **"No."**)

- Why do you feel we should hire you? (Speaks to **"Why."**)

Congratulations, I know that was time consuming. But now that you have a better sense of what you bring to the table of an interview, I hope you are energized not only by your sense of accomplishment, but also by the level of confidence you now have to posture yourself to *Lean Back* in your chair on that next interview.

Let's shift the focus from cultivating your "verbal" authentic story to setting the stage with your resume, cover letter and so much more as we move on to Chapter 5!

CHAPTER 5

The Virtual You

This chapter is designed to bring your body of work to life in the form of a resume, cover letter, 30-60-90, executive summary and in Follow Up correspondence, which, as you know, are an integral part of the search-for-employment process. Each document is your introduction to a potential employer, and the all-important post-interview thank you letter will contribute that positive impression.

The 30-60-90 and executive summary are optional. Their submission depends on what the job is calling for, and if you want to put in the added work to separate yourself from the rest of the candidates.

I remember a time when I was going up for a job and the hiring manager told me, "Just bring yourself to the interview." On a previous interview, I had my resume, executive summary and 30-60-90 available, just in case! This time I went with the flow. No prep! Until the night before my interview! A friend called. I told him about the interview and the hiring manager's comment. "Maureen," he said, "When was the last time you went on an interview without having on hand additional documentation to showcase who you are?"

"Never," I replied.

"Exactly! So why are you doing it now?"

What was my response? I stayed up all night to update and pull those documents together, and I'm so glad I did! Every one of my fellow applicants had them available, if needed. What I'm saying is, always be prepared to deliver and leave a lasting impression. Since the interviewer may not have captured all of your potential, it is important to share a leave-behind for reference.

Do not be overly concerned if you are a first-time job seeker or a returnee to the workforce. Focus on past experiences where you have demonstrated my pre-discussed proficiencies. Odds are you will pull together enough material to create a document that showcases who you are and what you are about.

From the minute you engage with a potential employer, consider it game on. Focus and follow through are extremely important here. When you fire on all cylinders, you will not only feel empowered, but you will also separate yourself from the other candidates.

Resumes

Your resume speaks to everything previously discussed and more. This document reveals to the skilled interviewer via details about past positions an individual's drive, work ethic, integrity and sense of ownership. Also, the resume showcases the applicant's go-above-and-beyond capabilities, for example, membership in an honor society, business, social or community club. Resumes need to pack a punch in a streamlined way. When you are creating yours, be mindful to include the following:

- **Logistics, including personal information:** List name, address, cellular number, email address, LinkedIn link and website if you have one. Interviewers will need to reach you. List both home and mobile numbers. Should you be among the employed, do not provide your current work email. It is super easy to create a new professional, private and free email address.

- **Professional summary** goes right under logistics. Yours should include a snapshot about who you are and what drives you. Also, it is important to use action verbs that speak to your skills. Some examples are:

  o Analytical

  o Creative

  o Determined

  o Formulated

  o Managed

  o Mentored

  o Negotiated

  Here, in the professional summary, list experiences that highlight your achievements, and drive home what you want your potential employer to know about you.

- **Professional experience**, a.k.a. work history. This category examines the nuts and bolts that demonstrate work ethic, behavior, communication style, etc. List all employers in chronological order starting with most recent. Include the company name, address and dates of tenure. List your position/title, responsibilities and accomplishments.

  Keep in mind, we have all developed a need for immediate gratification. Be brief and to the point when writing about your accomplishments in this section and make certain you link impact to every experience.

- **Education** is straightforward. Place the highest degree at the top. List the name of the institution, location, degree earned and your GPA. You need not include dates. A highlight here would also include any awards, recognitions, professional affiliations and honor societies.

- **Skills:** This section of your resume demonstrates to potential employers additional acquired abilities that may bode well for that particular position.

  o *Soft skills* speak to personality traits and habits that include communication style, emotional intelligence and time-management capabilities. Examples would include, but are not limited to, adaptability, creativity, empathy, integrity, open-mindedness and positive attitude.

  o *Hard skills* focus the interviewer on your technical abilities acquired, including any certifications. Examples would include, but are not limited to, additional languages spoken, database management, programming languages, and software proficiency.

Cover Letter

Ok, let's roll up our sleeves for this one. This is where you capture what you have learned from research done on the corporate website, as well as, by having a complete understanding of what the job description calls for.

Got that? This is so important it is worth reiterating. The meat of your cover letter can be pulled from the actual job description. For example, if the position requires a person with strong communication skills, then you provide a comment that reflects your proficiency with communication. *BAM!*

The mechanics of the cover letter should list your logistical information name, address, contact telephone number and email address as the letterhead.

Then it's back to grade school to recall the proper way to construct a business letter. Date on the upper left-hand side followed by the hiring manager's name, title and address. Your salutation goes below that, followed by the substance of the cover letter and closing.

Let's talk about the substance! It includes the opening, body and the closing. Within those confines are distinct entities that address the what, how and why. When I talk about the "what," I am referencing the *opening* of the cover letter. After your salutation, you will start your letter with an opening. This opening can literally make or break you.

It must be creative enough to hold the interviewer's attention, and it must speak to either who you are or what strengths you bring to the table. It must also specify the job you are applying for, and how you learned about that job. Be specific! Was it from LinkedIn or a search engine or a friend in the company?

The next paragraph is called the *body*. It highlights the "how." How does your experience align with what the company is looking for? To answer that question you must know your audience. You must research what they are looking for in a candidate.

This is the section where you translate your strengths by extrapolating qualifications already established on your resume. Be mindful of wordiness. Convey this information in a succinct way.

To clarify my point, let's make-believe. Let's pretend you are in a helicopter looking down at your accomplishments. All you have achieved in business or other areas fills your vision. What top qualities are visualized consistently and what accomplishments match the potential job description? What you bring to the table becomes crystal clear. You know who you are. Hence, the body shows the "how" of your accomplishments.

Incorporate your behind-the-scenes talents to produce a desired outcome here in the body of the cover letter. Show your interviewer what you are capable of.

And the *closing* should bring home the "why" you are a good fit for that position. It should summarize your qualifications and intentions and open the door for feedback and next steps.

Your cover letter allows the potential employer to see how polished and professional you are. On the other side of the spectrum, it allows you to sell your past accomplishments, and tie them into why those accomplishments would bring added success to that given company.

30-60-90

Simply stated, this is a document that demonstrates you have thought about the potential job to the point that you have laid out what you will do within the next 30 days, 60 days and 90 days of employment. Remember, the hiring manager is looking for a qualified candidate who is proactive and ready to lean into this new job. What better way to exemplify job readiness? And here's another plus! With your 30-60-90, you are already establishing a time commitment. Within each bracket of time specified on this document you will want to clearly state your goals and objectives. Be mindful; it doesn't have to be a novel. Bullet points succinctly show your hiring manager you have taken the time to step into the position and make decisions on how you will move forward.

By now, you should see this document talks about being accountable and proactive. It sets clear limits while allowing flexibility to grow.

Executive Summary

An executive summary is a document that houses additional details to complement your resume. In my opinion, it should house the following elements:

1. **Summary statement**: This houses 5 to 10 bullet points on who you are and what you want the interviewer to know about you. For example, when I was interviewing for a sales job, I put on my summary page that I was a former social worker with a Master's degree in Behavioral Science. I wanted them to know that because as a salesperson, I would need to uncover the needs of the client to shift their thinking. As a social worker, that was my job. Making that reveal fit nicely. It separated me from the rest. Understand? Your past experiences, although they may not be in the same genre, can bode well for a given job, and actually separate you from the pack.

2. **WIIFT:** You may be familiar with the acronym WIIFM, What's In It For Me? When you are interviewing, you should include a page with "WIIFT": What's In It For Them. Page 2 should demonstrate what you will bring to the team. Again, bullet points are the way to go here. For example, if the job is calling for the ability to be agile and you have experience in that arena, then you can put something to the effect of "experience with change management" or "flexible to change."

3. **Personal style:** I would encourage you to go online and take tests that will enable you to know you your leadership style, personality traits and aptitude. This is a great way to show you have gone above and beyond to demonstrate self-awareness and embody a thirst for knowledge around what makes you, you.

   I actually took a test on leadership. My test revealed I am a Participative Leader, the type of leader who accepts input from one or more group members when making decisions and solving problems, the type of leader who retains the final say when decisions are made. Group members tend to be encouraged and motivated by this style of leadership. It often leads to more effective and accurate decisions since no leader can be an expert in every area. I actually added that statement to my executive summary.

4. **LEANBACK™ Proficiencies:** I would like you to add a page to executive summary about your proficiencies. You don't need to include them all. I would look at the job description, and align a few of them to call out how you mastered that proficiency.

5. **Action plan:** This is where you could place your 30-60-90-day plan. Again, bullet points are key to highlight the direction you will take if given the job.

FOLLOW UP CORRESPONDENCE:

And last, but clearly important, is your follow-up correspondence. Letter writing has fallen off the face of the earth with the advent of computers, but, it's still so nice to receive a written letter of gratitude.

There are two schools of thought. There are those who prefer the tactile approach, where they can see, touch and feel a letter of thanks, and those who prefer to send a letter of gratitude via email. Both work very well. Just make sure you do one or the other!

Within that letter of thanks, and without being boastful, you should include a brief synopsis of why you are the perfect fit for that job. Explain how grateful you are for your time with them.

Create a foundation of integrity.

How are you feeling at this point? Has your mindset shifted from a reactive stance to a responsive stance? I said this statement earlier and need to bring it back into the light. "Do you speak "to" something, or do you speak "of" something?

In my layers of deep thinking, I find this statement to be profound. When you speak "to" something, there's not much thought or knowledge needed. It is similar to scratching the surface with general commentary. But when you speak "of" something, you are truly providing intellectual insight. Speaking "to" something and "of' something are both needed from time to time but for our purposes, and in order to *Lean Back* on the interview, you will want to be prepared to speak *of your* accomplishments. I hope at this point you are feeling a purposeful intent to imagine, inspire and ignite movement to the opportunities facing you today!

As I look back and reflect on all the new learnings in your "virtual briefcase," including:

- Self-reflection
- PERSPECTIVE with body language
- Researching insights in the Green Zone and Blue Zone
- LEANBACK™ proficiencies

- SCAN™'s
- Setting the stage with resumes, cover letters, 30-60-90's, executive summary's and follow-up correspondence

I ask you to pause and reflect on all you have learned.

OK, it's the time you've been preparing for. The Interview. The next chapter will open your eyes to every type of interview you could potentially face and how to navigate these interviews with confidence to create impact. Let's go!

CHAPTER 6:

The Interview

You made it! The day is here. And you, my friend, are ready to relax, deliver and ace a post-*Lean Back* employment interview. Congratulations!

I cannot tell you how excited I am at the thought of you sitting for that interview. You've come a long way! You've understood, absorbed, and practiced the "how-to" required to succinctly and eloquently reveal yourself, and your LEANBACK™ proficiencies to the interviewer. Knowledge has replaced anxiety. You feel secure in your thinking. You are ready!

As you *"Lean Back"* in the chair, as your voice resonates with confidence you eagerly share *why* you are the best candidate for the job! And there is a plus! If my words have seeped into the deepest recess of your mind, you will hear a tiny voice reminding you to, "Speak *of* your accomplishments!" It works every time!

This scenario will soon become a reality. As your mentor, your guide via *Lean Back*, I will be with you in spirit. How will you do? "You will blow them out of the water."

But I digress! There is more to learn! Are you with me? Metaphorically speaking, employment interviews come in all shapes and sizes. At one end of the spectrum there is the **Traditional Face-to-Face Interview**. This is conducted by a hiring manager, fellow colleagues or by a recruiter representing the company.

On the other end of the spectrum and is currently the option of choice due to the COVID virus, is the **Online Interview**. This takes place at the applicant's home or office. The interview is usually completed via Google Hangout, Microsoft Teams or Skype.

There are other types of interviews, whether face-to-face or virtual. Here is what you can expect:

- **The One-on-One Interview:** This is an interview where you are in the room, either virtual or in person, with the hiring manager or someone from the company (or a recruiter representing the company) to determine if you are a good fit for the job.

- **The Panel Interview:** This is conducted by a group of two or more company associates who will fire questions at the candidate. If you haven't read my book and you participate in this type of interview, the format may be overwhelming.

   I don't want to intimidate you; I want to prepare you. And I want you to think about the word "focus." If you focus on knowledge gained from the pages of this book, if you have absorbed the meaning of LEANBACK™ proficiencies and SCAN™, and if you have finished the self-help exercises sprinkled throughout these pages…any questions directed at you will be met with a SCAN™ of why you are the best person for the job.

   To better prepare you for the search of employment let me introduce you to a variety of business interviews to which you may be subjected.

- **The Group Interview:** Competition is the key word here. The hiring company hopes to separate the best from the rest by having two or more candidates showcase their LEANBACK™ proficiencies in an open forum. Should you partake in such an interview, the interviewer may bombard you with questions, but there is no need to feel anxious! You have researched the company, its leaders, mission and culture. You are prepared! Do not permit yourself to feel intimidated by this format.

Every bit of knowledge you have gleaned from my words and from the self-help exercises included in *Lean Back* has increased your confidence. Your ability to project yourself, and the LEANBACK proficiencies you bring, to the table, have been tested via written and verbal exercises. And you know what you are getting into! So go for it! And have no regrets!

- **The Phone Interview:** Do not let this seemingly easy style of interviewing fool you. It is not merely a phone screen, as some have said. It is step one in a two-step process. It is your introduction to a potential employer, your first impression! So, put a smile in your voice, and dazzle the interviewer with your proficiencies.

  During my time as an interviewer, I observed many candidates who did not take step one seriously. Not one of them made it to step two, the all-important face-to-face interview! Do not make that mistake! Give step one everything you've got!

  Actually, I find the phone interview to be the easiest of all interviews. It affords the candidate the opportunity to use the format, to share his/her stories, as one would do during an open-book test. What could be easier?

- **The Skype and Google Hangout:** These interview sites are becoming more and more utilized, especially in light of the COVID pandemic. You sit in front of your computer and log onto the assigned site. On screen, you will see the interviewer as though they were sitting in the room with you.

  A callout here! Make sure your desk and background are clean, clear and organized. Remember! Aside from your proficiencies, an interviewer will pick up on your surroundings. Portray the image you want him/her to remember.

Be effer-present!

That brings me to a non-verbal influence that can change the interview dynamics from good to bad without a word being spoken, the physical image projected via attire. It's simple: dress for the job you want. While you do not need to break your budget, choose well. A first impression, and that is what you are creating, is a one-time opportunity to provide the interviewer with positive reasons to remember you. Proper attire is a plus!

It is important to call out your attire for a Skype or Google Hangout interview. You may not be sitting in the room with your potential employer, but he/she might ask you to stand up. If you are buttoned up from the waist to neck yet unbuttoned from the waist down, the flush on your face will be met with an embarrassed you. And you may have soured a positive first impression! So, dress appropriately and completely. Right down to your shoes. They may be checked out as well.

Rehearsal Makes Perfect

Now is the time to practice with "mock" interviews with friends and family. If you have not done so, please get out there. Rehearse your story with friends and family or practice verbalizing your SCAN in front of the bathroom mirror. You must be comfortable with your words when speaking at the interview. There should be no smirks or filler words, including; "like, ""uhhh," or "ahhh" or any mispronounced words when delivering your story. Practice is the one way to accomplish that goal.

If you recall my chapter on self-reflection, I talked about this. It is not only important to self-reflect on how you did on former interviews, it is important to raise your level of awareness around your non-verbal cues as well. What you want to present to a potential employer is the complete picture, knowledge, appearance and personality!

And lastly, you may think of recording yourself. This will allow you to determine if your story is succinct and impactful and to hear if excessive use of filler words is diminishing the effectiveness and impact of your story.

Timeliness encompasses several areas. Make sure you are on time for each and every scheduled employment interview. And if you should arrive 15 minutes before your interview is scheduled, realize you are late. Check both your method of transportation and the time it will take to get there, including unanticipated traffic to ensure a timely arrival. Make it a point to arrive at least 30 minutes in advance of your interview. This allows you time to relax, meditate and reflect on key points you want to bring to light. It also shows the interviewer you are in complete control of time management.

Timeliness, also, speaks to the sense of urgency you demonstrate in response to any questions the hiring manager may ask. When you act promptly and without delay, you demonstrate you are all-in organized, and that you have a clear mindset about the outcome.

External stimuli may shift your focus and throw you off your game. So, no cellphones at the interview! If you must bring one, put it on silent mode and away from your vision to avoid any distractions. Keep pens with clickers out of reach to avoid unintentionally clicking the pen as you answer questions.

You may also want to move your keys to a place where you can't fidget with them. But not in your pocket! You may subconsciously put your hands there and jiggle them.

Proof-of-concept, my newly coined definition, speaks to what you are bringing with you, to an interview. Before arriving, research all there is to know about the hiring firm, its management, culture and policies. Also, you will want to know how many people will be interviewing you so that you may provide them with copies of your resume, executive summary and/or 30-60-90-day plan.

Disseminating this information to each interviewer will allow you to leave a lasting positive impression. Interviewers, as mentioned earlier, may not capture everything. By providing them with proof-of-concept, they will be able to review your candidacy at will. That may bring to life other aspects they didn't previously notice. It could prompt a second look at your resume. It is a win/win move!

Make sure you bring enough material and be sure to house it in a polished way. Coordinate your colors and type of paper and house it in a folder. I have also given out this information on a thumb drive, just to be different! Creativity may get you noticed. It may set you apart from other applicants. If you feel the urge, go with it! It can't hurt and may help!

Brain freeze: This talks to a temporary lapse in memory. An interviewer asks a question. You experience brain freeze. You panic. Oh no! What to do? Knowing how prepared you are, I'm sure this won't happen, but if it does, the best way to combat a brain freeze is to cultivate more time to answer a question.

Diversion tactics come in handy here. Tell the interviewer you want to make sure you understood the question being asked. Then repeat it back to him/her. This gives your brain the ability to muster up an answer. This will prompt the interviewer to add to that question. End result, you have demonstrated accountability and authenticity because you truly want to answer that question accurately.

Other stall tactics include complimenting the question by saying, "That's a great question!" Your brain is amazing at rallying; you will only need a few seconds to formulate a given answer. Lastly, don't be afraid to tell the interviewer that you would like a minute to think about the question.

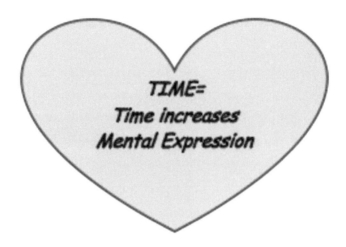

Check in! This term is so important! It changes the entire context of the interview. When you "check in" with your interviewer, you are simply making sure they are engaged and interested in what you are saying. For example, you are sharing a SCAN of when you had completed a problematic task. By checking in and saying, "Does that make senses to you?" You are pulling the interviewer into your world for a deeper engagement.

Other ways to check in with an interviewer are through the use of the following questions: "Have I answered that question or do you need more information?" "Do you feel what I have shared so far fits with what you are looking for?" "Is there anything else I can share to demonstrate my ability to do the job well?"

Curtain call, also known as a final bow in theater lingo, can apply nicely here. The interview is almost over. Your interviewer will close out the interview with a final question to you. They will ask if you have any questions for them.

It is very important to have at least two questions ready. These questions can range from gaining a better understanding of the corporate structure to gaining a better understanding of what a typical day at the firm looks like. You can ask what they like most about the company or about challenging aspects of the given job. The important focus here is to be authentic. And all in! Don't leave that interview without understanding what the job is about, how they feel you did and what the next steps are.

At this point in time, you should feel really good about your position during the interview. You have reflected, driven inwardly to understand your proficiencies and pulled them together in a succinct story highlighting *you*.

Let this book be the beginning of a new self-reflective journey. May you always have thirst for self-enlightenment and the drive to be the best you can be. Remember, life happens on purpose. You lose out on every opportunity you don't take advantage of. Could 'a, would 'a, should 'a applies here! Do not let that be you! So, I wish you the best as you *Lean Back* to a career of a lifetime!

As I close out this chapter, I'd like to create some forward thinking for when you get that dream job. As you start your journey of employment, I want you to always reflect on who you are and what qualities and proficiencies you bring to that career. And know your brand!

Personal brand, is a fancy way of saying, what do you want to be known for? The answer lies within you. You must be authentic; you must know and understand the key qualities you consistently drive with. If you copy someone else, you lose originality.

Creating a personal brand brings the qualities you possess to life, and it should be conveyed in a concise way. Many corporations are encouraging employees to create their elevator pitch, a mini personal brand, so that each employee will be able to convey a succinct story of who they are and what their story is in an abbreviated amount of time.

In my opinion, this is a marketing perception of who you are. As for me, I value personal branding, but truly believe it is incumbent on the employee, and not the employer, to define his/her professional self and strengths via this method.

CHAPTER 7:

The Afterglow

The afterglow.

A sense of accomplishment and pride. You have done your work to prepare and promote your story. You feel good! Now what? Do you bask in the glory of an interview well done? Well, not just yet!

Now that the interview is behind you, let the afterglow resonate by reflecting on that interview. If you recall the lessons from chapter 1 on self-reflection, you learned to be aware of your body language through the acronym, P.E.R.S.P.E.C.T.I.V.E™. You have also attained an inner focus that enables you to review the audios of completed interviews. But you must remain focused, purposeful and poised.

It is important to reflect on the overarching questions that were asked of you during the interview. It is equally important to revisit the job description so that you can correlate and summarize how you demonstrated why you are the right person for the job. And finally, you will want to re-capture insights gained about the company and or job that was of interest to you. If needed, utilize the proficiency model, LEANBACK™ from Chapter 2. Write down two to three examples of what the given company was looking for next to the key proficiencies.

Now, let us take a look at how you can pull together needed information for follow-up correspondence. Simply re-capture notes on the job description that the company was looking for in the LEANBACK™ Proficiency. Then notate the post interview reflection and insights gained from the interview. Take a look below:

- **Job Description:** Excellent communication and interpersonal skills

- **LEANBACK™ Proficiency:** Communication

- **Post-interview recap:**

  o Demonstrated the ability to develop relationships quickly with clients by listening and uncovering needs so they will feel heard.

  o Detailed written communication skills evidenced by timely and consistent emails to the leadership team, so they remain abreast of customer insights.

  o Excellent presentation and negotiation skills shared through examples of presenting the features and benefits of product X to a customer. By being prepared to address their objections, I was able to close the deal.

- **Insights gained**: I loved learning about the company training program for new employees and how it brings to light the various career opportunities I can eventually pursue.

I truly believe self-reflection is a life skill.

Now that you have captured salient points from the interview, you will need to be mindful of time and space. When I speak to "time", I am referencing time to follow up. When I speak to "space", I am referencing your post-interview presence. Let's talk about that!

I may sound a little old fashioned, but one thing that never gets old is follow up. What is crucial here is that you are mindful that time is of the essence. Once you complete your interview, you will want to send a "thank you note" to everyone who interviewed you, individually.

A thank you note is an email or written note thanking the hiring manager and their associates for their time. Please send these notes individually and not as a group email. The thank you note also conveys a lot about you;

your sense of urgency, follow-through or lack-there-of, organization skills and yes, communication skills. The timeline to send your thank you note, in my opinion, should be between one-hour post interview up to and no later than twenty-four hours later.

A thank you note not only conveys gratitude but can remind the hiring manager why you are the right person for the position. So, take a look at the post-interview insights you captured, and weave that into your thank you note. Keep it short and sweet and be sure to include your contact information so he or she has your number on hand. Again, "time" is crucial!

Follow-through in a timely manner will truly demonstrate your interest with a given job. On the other hand, I must share with you the delicate balance of follow-up through "space". I mentioned earlier that you need to be mindful of "time" and "space."

When I reference space, I am talking to the amount of times you reach out the that given manager/company to obtain updates regarding their decision. Stalking has never proven to be a welcoming experience. Give then space!

The silence post-interview can be deafening. I get it! We all want to be wanted but being overly eager and or pushy could become disconcerting to the hiring manager. Your actions could even hurt your chances of getting that job.

So, how do you keep your presence once your thank you note has been sent?

Simple. By sending additional correspondence in a timely way. Below, is a timeline of correspondence that I have found to be welcoming.

One hour up to twenty-four hours post interview: Send thank you note.

One-week post interview: It is at this time, if you haven't heard back from the hiring manager, recruiter or company yet, you will craft a "follow-up" note and send it to the hiring manager. Set your calendar to remind you. A follow-up note is a way to gain insights on where they are in the process. Please remember, you are not the only candidate that is interviewing for the position. And, that given manager has a day job as well. So, be patient. You may still be in the running. Don't lose hope!

The concept of the follow- up note is to convey your continued high level of interest for that given position. it also allows you to ask if any additional information is needed to demonstrate your ability to do the job well. And finally, ask the hiring manager if he or she has any updates to share at this time. Again, the follow-up email should be similar to the thank you note in that it is short and sweet.

Three weeks post interview: At this point you should have received some type of correspondence or follow up from the company. But, if you haven't, you may want to send a "feedback note". This note should follow the others, and be short and sweet. It will potentially give you an opportunity to gain insights into what you did well and where the opportunities for growth are. You can call out, on this note, that you wanted to reach out to see if a decision has been made, reiterate your excitement for the position and ask to set up a brief connection to obtain feedback. If by chance you did not get that position, you can utilize the feedback note as well to gain an understanding of what you could have done differently.

Nonetheless, whether you get the job or not, you should send a gracious email thanking them for their time. If the answer was a no, please do not represent yourself in a negative way. You do not know what the future brings and if you burn bridges, you may miss out on any future opportunities they may have.

There is one other note I must bring to you attention. And that is the "thank you- but-note." I always encourage my clients to cast a wide net when interviewing. Meaning? Apply to many positions that match your qualifications. You may find yourself in a gracious spot where you are offered a dream job while waiting to hear about another job.

There are two ways to approach this; If you choose to take that dream job, please communicate and let the other companies know how thankful you are for their time and enjoyed learning about the company…, but… have decided to accept another offer. Another way to approach this is to communicate the offer to the other companies you are interviewing with. Let them know you have another offer. That said, tell them you truly admire the values and mission of the company and would love to hear back before deciding.

Good impressions have lasting results

This chapter, the Afterglow, as you can see, is all about communication and setting expectations. As you grow from a professional perspective, always know that life is about the journey and not the destination.

Unfortunately, not all companies you interview with will respond with a decision. I don't agree with their lack of response. But it is what it is. You need to be prepared. Always know there is a path for you. Always, rely on the belief that you proficiencies will be a great fit for a given company one day. Keep the faith You are ready!

Lean Back in your chair, share your story with confidence and belief in the next interview. My good wishes go with you.

Perhaps, we will meet again on the pages of my next book. Till then enjoy the fruits of your business endeavors!

Live the sweetness of balance by breathing in life; both the length and depth!

May good luck and happiness be your best friends!
Mo